THE FACE IN THE WELL

Rebecca Watts was born in Suffolk in 1983 and currently lives in Cambridge. A selection of her poetry was included in *New Poetries VI* (2015). Her debut collection *The Met Office Advises Caution* (2016) was a Poetry Book Society Recommendation and was shortlisted for the 2017 Seamus Heaney Centre Prize. Her second collection, *Red Gloves*, was published in 2020 and won a Gladstone's Library Writers-in-Residence Award.

Also by Rebecca Watts

Red Gloves, 2020
Elizabeth Jennings: New Selected Poems (editor), 2019
The Met Office Advises Caution, 2016

REBECCA WATTS

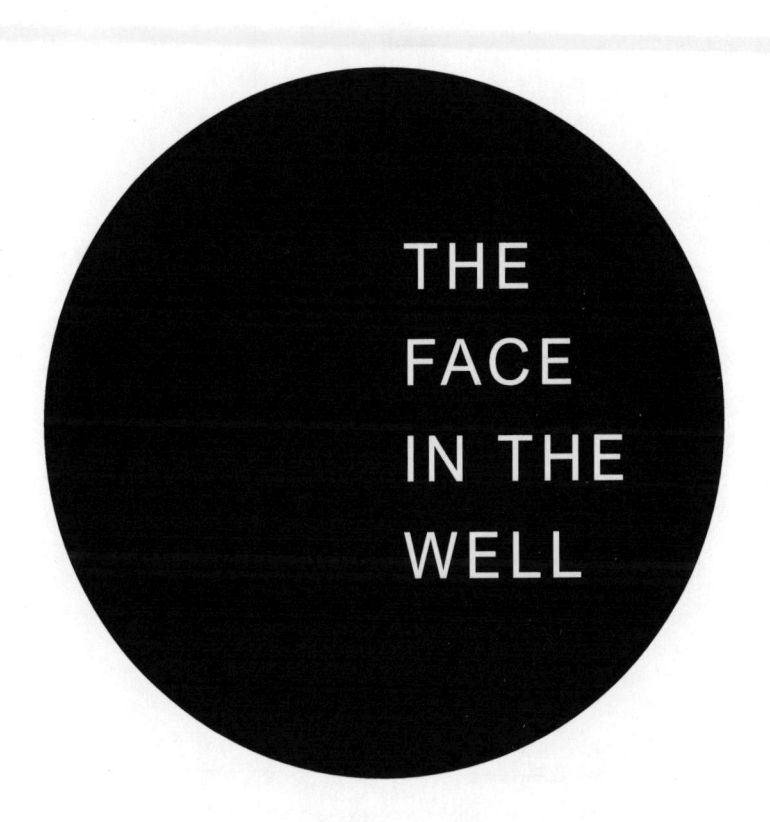

THE
FACE
IN THE
WELL

CARCANET POETRY

First published in Great Britain in 2025 by
Carcanet
Alliance House, 30 Cross Street
Manchester, M2 7AQ
www.carcanet.co.uk

Text copyright © Rebecca Watts 2025

The right of Rebecca Watts to be identified as the author
of this work has been asserted in accordance with the
Copyright, Design and Patents Act of 1988; all rights reserved.

A CIP catalogue record for this book is
available from the British Library.

ISBN 978 1 80017 458 0

Book design by Andrew Latimer, Carcanet
Typesetting by LiteBook Prepress Services
Printed in Great Britain by SRP Ltd, Exeter, Devon

The publisher acknowledges financial
assistance from Arts Council England.

CONTENTS

Private No Access	9
Song	10
Hazelling the Field	11
Soundings I: 1987	12
The Landscapes of My Childhood	13
Autobiographia Literaria	14
Women Poets (in Order of Preference)	15
'Disposing of dead rodents is a man's job' (Mumsnet forum)	16
Personal Effects	17
Victoriana	18
I Want to Be the Orange	20
Concentrate	21
There are some things your parents can't teach you;	22
Soundings II: Waiting for Mary Poppins	23
Annie, with Starlings	24
The Miniaturist	25
The Old Mill	26
When my sister,	27
The Wandering Albatross	28
The Face in the Well	29
Soundings III: En Route to Great Yarmouth	30
The Mainland	31
White Lies	32
She Wishes for the Cliffs of Devon	33
All My Joy	34
Baroque	35
The Young Comedian Enrols at Clown School	36
Soundings IV: Stations	37
Woman seeks	38
Lessons from Lenny	39

OM	40
Four in the Morning	41
Leaving	42
Shark	43
Running the Planet Trail	44
Wolf Moon	45
At Home with Emily Brontë	46
Heptonstall	47
Procrastination Island	48
The Reptile House	50
The Great Disappointment	51
That	52
The Garden	54
The Drum	55
Multiverse Valentine	56
What Mouse Said	57
Buttermere	58
Joining the Spiders	59
Entropy	60
Hawarden Park, Dawn	61
Notes and Acknowledgements	63

THE FACE IN THE WELL

PRIVATE NO ACCESS

The animal in me is padding through woods in the rain,
    poking her nose in rabbit holes,
forging a channel through the bluebell sea
    which quivers in her wake.

The animal in me is rooting out spiders and insects,
    scuffing rich dirt beneath a dripping oak,
close and low-down tracking the scent of musk
    which spells out the name of her kind.

The birches' eyes are on her and she does not care,
    for she has the world on her side, the green
harkening follow-me world
    where every thing alive is permitted

and everything is alive. Her ears prick – momentary –
    at the crunch of gravel as someone about-heels
in deference to the sign. She runs
    and the wild-garlic stars burst open.

SONG

    Dolphin is the soul
before the world gets to her

    joy's missile
shadowing the hull

    dipping and rising
till we see what she's made of

    smiling and whole
saying *come on, dive in!*

    Dolphin is the soul
before all life's stuff

    chairless and deskless
and wild as the air

    a swimming song
oh happy child!

    I met her once
upon a bright blue day

    before the fishermen
rolled out their nets

HAZELLING THE FIELD

Let's take a knife
and our differences
down to the hazel wood.

Two strokes each
converts to four
stakes in the ground.

Let's run these round
with rope to make
a ring, then step

in. Let's box. Or let's
bow before a sacred
court. Either way

we'll agree that justice
should be outsourced,
or the fight fenced off,

so our grievances
won't grow into
feuds, battles, wars.

SOUNDINGS I: 1987

The milk bottles are rattling on the tray.
The paper straws are bobbing in the holes.
I shut my eyes and wish myself away
from Smelly Betty and Unkind Peter.

THE LANDSCAPES OF MY CHILDHOOD

The landscapes of my childhood were cosy:
stopped-clock church towers nestled among oak and ash,
a static river mirroring a static sky.

I am still among the landscapes of my childhood.
When I walk out in the mornings, hardly a thing moves:
a squirrel, a magpie, a few pigeons mostly.

I'd like to arrive in the landscapes of my adulthood –
to feel precarious, scared even, at where I've come to,
its heights and precipices and many shadowed crevices.

Large mammals likely thrive in the landscapes of my adulthood –
gorillas and elephants and giraffes, all wholly
real, not merely actors in a showcase for a zoo,

and each day is as striking as a zebra there, and as clear,
and the flora abounds, very hungry, and grows huge.
In the landscapes of my adulthood I think I'll meet you,

who'll tell me things I don't already know, and be reassured
by my memories of the landscapes of my childhood
as we hunker and sing shanties in our cabin in the storm.

I am still among the landscapes of my childhood.

AUTOBIOGRAPHIA LITERARIA

Teachers
I adored who
would not love me! Misses
Warwick and Charlesworth – young, pretty
women

made of
curls and white musk –
how I cried, wanting to
be like them! and how my crying
made them

hate me!
so instead of
understanding they showed
me to the reading corner, where
cross-legged

I sat
facing the wall
of books, blocking the screams
from the playground, teaching myself
to lose

myself
in the other
worlds, which some faraway
kind person wanted me to know
are there

WOMEN POETS (IN ORDER OF PREFERENCE)

Mrs Dedication

Would you just look at her –
neat hair parted centre, pious smile;
a real doll.

She took care of him –
collected and copied out his works in fairest hand;
later penned a few love lyrics of her own.

Eccentric spinster

Oh, something happened to her
way back in school –
a fellow in the bushes doing what he shouldn't.
She's a clerk now –

types her poems winter evenings
with a beaker of tonic for company.
Some of them are even funny.

Mad girl

You could tell from the get-go she was one
to steer clear of – not a beauty
exactly, but the way she kept on looking
made it tough to look away.

Latchkey for a necklace. Lightning
moods – would trash anything sooner than give it up.
Walked herself onto the stake.
Still burns.

'DISPOSING OF DEAD RODENTS IS A MAN'S JOB' (MUMSNET FORUM)

*

My friend's daughter in a sweet floral dress
poking at a rat the size of her head

as it lies stiff on the drain cover, its sneer
chronicling the horrible ecstasy of the poisoned.

*

My friend, her mother, donning marigolds,
doubling black sacks and trowelling the corpse inside

while speculating about its time of death
with the nonchalance of a TV pathologist.

PERSONAL EFFECTS

My mother keeps parts of me under her bed.
Parts she gave; parts
she took back.

Folded into tissues
and tucked inside envelopes
like little wage packets

are twists of my hair, my teeth,
my bracelet from the hospital –
things I never asked for,

whose capture
I didn't resist, and above which,
dark nights, she tosses and turns.

I don't miss them,
since they have been replaced
with new hair, new teeth,

and I could buy myself a bracelet
any time. But when I see her sometimes
seeing me

smiling for a photo
or tightening my ponytail
or taking off my watch and placing it on the windowsill

I wonder if she's considering
claiming other relics
that one day could remind us both who we are.

VICTORIANA

They bought six plots
when DAUGHTER *FELL ASLEEP*. Tragedy
begets morbidity.

Two graves, with space
for three in each. *TOGETHER*
THROUGHOUT ETERNITY.

When MOTHER died,
she was laid beside – age
to balance beauty –

and a second
polished marble heart
inscribed *IN SACRED MEMORY*.

FATHER tended
to both with care – brought flowers
each anniversary –

but made the most
of his extra years, and never
seemed melancholy.

When his time came
he shocked us with his wish to be
burned: contrary.

We buried the urn
at the foot of Mam's grave, and tried
not to think about loyalty.

Now us three boys
have married and moved, no one
visits the cemetery

so the matter
of who should lie with whom
shan't trouble posterity.

And the resting bones
shall be left alone, oppressed
by the good earth only.

I WANT TO BE THE ORANGE

I want to be the orange.
The blueberry has merits –
special powers relative
to its size (a *superfruit*!)
– but is too easily lost,
tiny, accidentally
squashable, dusty, inter
rupted by its husky stalk,
soft, hard, sharp, sour, out-of-time.

I want to be the orange.
I want to be generous
and tough, vibrant and yielding,
delighted and protected,
largely idle, throwable
and catchable, and beaming
all the while – able to spare
my golden afterglow, so
sure am I that I was there.

CONCENTRATE

Could I buy this   my room to myself   by the hour

you at your meeting   and nothing at all from the house

boiler   clocks   the pigeons in the roof all

taciturn   all rhythm abandoned   carpet socks

the front gate fastened   the neighbours away

washing machine idle   the table

swept of festivities whiteboard   wiped clean

just the morning and me   the only one around

to ask   could I buy this   and what would it cost

THERE ARE SOME THINGS YOUR PARENTS CAN'T TEACH YOU;

they grip too tight. So it's a woman from
the other end of the village (Sonia,
apparently) who's jogging along
behind the purple bike with the fat white
tyres on the field next to the school this
sunny Saturday – her palm steadying
the back of the saddle, her fingers curled
beneath – panting encouraging words

to the small, shy girl in the red tracksuit
who grips the handlebars like a pilot
pushing off from tarmac, legs spinning like
propellers, her gaze so completely fixed
on what's ahead that she doesn't sense
the stranger's hand has already let go.

SOUNDINGS II: WAITING FOR MARY POPPINS

Rules and cleanliness
are all we want:
to know where we are,
where *naughty* is.

Security in strictures.
A chance to please.
Order and routine.
Bread and jam at five.

ANNIE, WITH STARLINGS

Running on noise and velcro and diggers
and drop-offs and laundry and lost coats and pick-ups
and stories and bath-times and weekend wellies,
you don't give a thought to the miscarriages.

At the end of the garden you toss the remains of a crumble
to the birds without hearing *waste waste waste*
and the cool smooth sides of the dish
feel nice, its emptiness.

THE MINIATURIST

Esme draws a picture
but it's only a whisper –
the pencil barely touches the paper

as she ghost-traces a box with a triangle roof
three First-Aid-crossed windows
and a door with a dot for a handle

and beside that a lollypop tree
and on the opposite side a thin chimney
with a pigtail of smoke.

None of the houses she's lived in
looked anything like this,
and still it's home –

where she must shrink right down
until she's only a speck,
invisible in the corner of the glass.

THE OLD MILL

What happened there,
down by the old mill,
they never tell.

Something about
a man and a girl
is the most you'll hear.

What's clear is that,
wishing the deed undone,
the villagers made the mill pay –

drove a stake through its heart
in the shape of a JCB,
whose wrecking claw

shredded the place
from roof to door. Now
only a part of one wall

and a couple of gear wheels
hang on at the edge of the pool.
Go down and you'll find it

where the water's ferrous
with rust, or blood,
depending how you're minded.

WHEN MY SISTER,

nonchalant as a teenager (though she's not yet nine), stomps
past the campsite café and jerks out a finger to stab

one of the big smooth buttons on the vender, without looking,
it is I, a bit behind and half skipping to keep up, who am

the primary witness to a miracle whose soundtrack
is the clunk, whirr and thud of its release and drop:

a can of Lilt

bedewed with condensation, new-born on the black felt
bed of the machine. We proclaim it the work of an angel,

and the best thing ever to befall our meagre lives.
Three decades later I'll be able still to resurrect the feeling –

wonder and awe; the instant, universal banishment of doubt.
And though we won't be talking, I'll want to text her straight away

to make it real again, and she'll reply straight back,
pulling over in a layby on the way home from the school run

just to say: *The Lilt! My god, the Lilt. How could I forget?*

THE WANDERING ALBATROSS

won't budge. Tired
of her name,
tired of travel
and the southern
blue, she sinks
into the patch
of land she's
found, and spreads
her windsurf wings
only to feel
the sun. She
won't meet her
mate of thirty
years again – so
much water under
the bridge. She'll
die here, and
nothing and no
one will care.
And that's all.

THE FACE IN THE WELL

As a child, I never went near a well.
Too dangerous, they said – so I stayed away,

played carefully at the courtyard's edge,
dragging my fingers through the unswept dust.

But one day I tired of the house's shadow,
the grey rectangle of the afternoon.

I stepped into the sun and felt its power
filter into me, drawing me on.

Rough brick grazed my palms as I leant over the side,
strained on tiptoes to peer into the gloom,

where I recognised a face, like mine but changed –
rounder, like the moon, neither young nor old,

just hanging brightly in the soft black sky
which stretched into the soundless universe.

Loneliness and fear and all the shame
that dutifully feeds them flowed away.

I didn't have to hear my voice thrown back
to understand the face was always there,

at home deep down, connected to the source,
needing a reflection to make it live.

SOUNDINGS III: EN ROUTE TO GREAT YARMOUTH

Can anybody actually hear me?
I'm shouting through the car's back window

while the others stand around in the layby laughing
at my act, which isn't an act at all.

THE MAINLAND

Folk on the mainland
are tightytighty.
Folk on the mainland
walk a rope.

No listening on the mainland,
only talking.
To walk while you talk
and to talk while you type.

What use for the mainland?
Polystyrene and mattresses.
Bad juju on the mainland.
Bad eating. Bad faith.

What use for the ocean?
For swallowing questions.
Who when why what NO:
shh shh on the shingle.

Conundrum: how to slip
through the mainland's fingers.
A few who have done this.
A few who have known.

What happens on leaving?
The end of the story.
The start of a new one:
wingbeats, wind.

WHITE LIES

      You wave your hands
shutter your eyes
      state it again
blame the weather

      little white lies
never hurt us
      did they? little
white lies never
      hurt anyone

SHE WISHES FOR THE CLIFFS OF DEVON

Had I south Devon's embattled cliffs,
Ablaze with gorse-bloom and salted light,
The sand and the schist and the chalk cliffs
Of rust and slate and softest white,
I would spread the cliffs under your feet:
But I, being here, have only ploughed fields;
I have spread ploughed fields under your feet;
Head south, love; beware the drag of ploughed fields.

ALL MY JOY

Robin is dead
no more shall sing
nor ruffle his wing
no more shall sing

Robin is dead
no more shall wait
at the garden gate
no more shall wait

Robin is dead
his soul has flown
but whither gone
oh whither gone

Robin is dead
and all my joy
my sweet bonny boy
and all my joy

BAROQUE

Let me be baroque in death as I've been practical in life.
Let six black-plumed stallions draw the black-gloss carriage
wherein my black-gloss casket rests upon a maple plinth
festooned with lilies – outrageously frilled and huge white
lilies exploding from every crevice, their syrupy
musk clogging the air for miles around. Let it halt all
deliveries. Let the golden trim of the vast black wheels
flash and wink as we roll by, let the mourners' wails fly
above the roofs of inappropriately mundane semis
where only grandpa doesn't doubt his seeing eyes.
Let the teenagers of the parish be absolved from Maths
and History and PE, and instead beat timpani, their pale
necks bowed to the heavy instruments, the pulse
recalling the slow-time march of an invading army,
while out in front a lone flautist draped in velvet
presages our coming with tones as dissonant and forsaken
as a freight train horn petitioning the night. Afterwards,
let there be rain: sudden and catastrophic rain
for a thousand days, washing all the pavements clean.

THE YOUNG COMEDIAN ENROLS AT CLOWN SCHOOL

At Clown School her face and her long limbs
are her five best assets. When the coach says
Take Up Space she eats the air
like it's Angel Delight, scooping its pink
peaks into her arms. She can do *Small* too,

like a wormcast on the beach at low tide,
and she can do *Frog*,
which is wider than *Jack-in-the-Box*.
Bravo! This kind of work
discharges from the soul; it can't be put back.

Back at real school her teachers are fit to burst.
You can wipe that look off your face right now,
one of them swipes, as she sinks into the seat
wearing her best *Hangdog*, chin tucked, brow knitted,
bottom lip stuck out. She's under his skin,

and she'd better get used to it
because it's going to be the same all her life.
Even when she's got a proper job there'll be people
who'll want to prevent her from shimmering
like moonlight on the sea;

who'll want to blot out the moon entirely,
finding her mute presence *too strong*,
her round face *too expressive*.

SOUNDINGS IV: STATIONS

I came to the Brontës rather late
for a girl of a bookish persuasion.
You christened your guinea pigs Emily and Charlotte.
My goldfish were called Egg and Bacon.

WOMAN SEEKS

educated or otherwise enlightened man with quick mind and strong arm for inspiring and harmonious lifetime experience. Must be excited, not diminished, by particular characteristics of woman (laser intelligence, pragmatism, emotional volatility, singing). Walking speed in excess of 3.5 mph essential. Must possess own toolbox and functioning automobile. Must manifest active appreciation of English Lake District, south-western coastline, cocker spaniels and donkeys. Must be able to count, weigh and measure reliably. Practical in the kitchen, lounge, bedroom and garden: can tell a radish from a rhododendron and, ideally, a mistlethrush from a long-tailed tit. Ability to troubleshoot basic IT issues while remaining temperamentally wedded to the analogue preferred. (Must not consider *Call of Duty* an appropriate source of recreation.) Should love reading without harbouring literary ambitions. Proficiency in guitar, banjo, ukulele or folk violin highly desirable. Tree surgeons, experimental archaeologists, sculptors and mechanical engineers are strongly encouraged to apply.

LESSONS FROM LENNY

Stop reading poetry. If you want to know
what love is, go
caretake a Bernese
while his owners bake under palm trees
in Castell de Ferro.

Feed him exactly what he's used to
and no more. Let him lead you
at a trot to all his choice places
and wait
while he sniffs the world anew.

In the house, notice how he keeps
you in sight without looking; how he sleeps
with his back against the stair
and jump-turns the second you appear.
Quieter than anyone you'll meet,

even before
you've pulled the soft rake through his fur
and caught the dark
candy floss of it in your palm,
he'll offer you his lion's paw.

When he drinks
it's a tsunami. What he thinks
is unknowable. When you scratch
behind his ears and lock eyes, feel how much
a minute's worth. How you don't flinch.

OM

Pull back the carpet
on last year's compost.
Amid the richness:
ratholes, a snakeskin;
the fetid carcass
of a wounded muntjac.

We grow our food
between such influences.
The body incorporates
what the mind refuses,

so there's a hint
of rat and snake
in all of us. Our kind
soft hearts spring
from moist darknesses,
the wasted ribcage.

FOUR IN THE MORNING

after Wisława Szymborska

The hour of round and round.
The hour from no to no.
The hour of unplucked strings.

The hour gnawed through to the grey bone.
The hour when god-knows-what emits a dusk-like glow.
The hour when shadowy branches drop their needles.
The hour of when-will-my-hands-regain-their-grasp.

The surgical hour.
Cruel, creeping.
Silent-spider hour; old friend.

Only the lost and hungry are awake at this hour.
Hedgehogs and foxes range about, knowing they'll sleep soon.
No one wins. Nobody receives
praise; cold comfort for the open-eyed.

LEAVING

We left in a hurry
and I had to leave
my solid-wood mahogany and spruce guitar.

They said to bring only what we could carry
and it would have taken both my arms
to protect it from knocks and scrapes as I would a baby –
for it too was made with love and in the belief it would last forever.

Now I'm more sorry
than I should say, to know I will never hold it again
and pluck the bass string and feel the low hum
travel through me, earthing me.

At night I crouch awake and worry
about the fire that melts and blackens and harries to ash
all the carefully crafted truths we once lived by
and which made life beautiful.

SHARK

may be lonely

                          so starved he bumps
                              another's nose

and can't tell the difference

                              moves slowly
          though quicker

              when the carcass falls

(may not feed again
                this year)

        wears loneliness
                            like a shark suit

and appears huge
              to cameras

        and pesky

              to his dumb   dead prey

flourishes
      in the dimmest reaches

     until his shark suit

              rots away

RUNNING THE PLANET TRAIL

2.8 billion miles still to go. Something
is slipping. Something pulls.

Under the dual carriageway I witness parallels:
my concrete hamstrings, its tattooed struts.

O east-west artery, shade me;
I can't take the heat.

I should've stopped at Mars with its anklet of beer cans and vapes.
I should've backtracked to Venus.

Yesterday in the cathedral I saw tourists with headphones
crawling all over St Frideswide's shrine

while on the north wall a map of Ukraine
beaconed its colours to anyone capable of feeling.

The prayer cards on the wrought-iron tree said 'My niece' and 'My godson'
and 'exam stress' and 'a hole in his heart'. The sun sloped in.

Light a candle while the soldiers bank and dive.
Light a hundred candles while they cover their ears.

Names, names, names. Knees, knees, knees.
How big and alive we are! And then.

Reprogramme the audio-guides. Pray to your god for a well,
a cooling rain. Should I go on?

In the lee of a fisherman, two young rabbits shiny with dew.
A collared dove some way past Jupiter.

WOLF MOON

On the eve of the full moon the woman cried.
I just want to be loved, she said
and curled up on the sofa like a wolf cub
who hasn't the foggiest idea she's no part wolf.

AT HOME WITH EMILY BRONTË

Ironing is her favourite task.
The rhythm and the steam

transport her to an outer state
more vivid than a dream –

a place of creased and crumpled hills,
a wet and heavy land

through which a burning body moves,
directed by her hand.

Each stroke a stride, the rugged earth
dissolves into a plain

whence she can touch the brooding clouds
and taste the coming rain.

This wide expanse, this untrod moor
she spreads out fresh each day

and, godlike, when she's done with it
she folds the world away.

HEPTONSTALL

O poets, o wives,
be done with words.
Ink leaks into blackened,
rain-soaked earth

and a pen takes ten lifetimes
to decompose.
I favour the flesh
of the lily, the rose,

which picks apart quickly
and rots and is gone.
No legacy message,
no guardian stone

like a shielding palm
round a delicate flame.
No pilgrimage site,
no date and no name:

just an honest hillside
at the edge of a moor
where no one comes knocking
on nobody's door.

PROCRASTINATION ISLAND

Some of us can't see the wood
for the piles of notes
obscuring the windows –

notes on paper,
in the making of which
the established view has had to be dismantled.

We try another tack,
bend our minds to an alternative approach,
but down on the beach

it's high-note tide,
the smooth and shiny stones all
lost beneath a swell of notes.

We construct an origami boat,
roll up notebooks for oars
and paddle staunchly to the horizon

where novel observations
are reeled aboard like minnows
and several drownings are recorded.

Those of us who make it back to shore
find much has changed since we set off –
even the words sound different now.

We chase meanings
down rabbit holes, tap into our Notes apps
where they might have gone,

a new note for every one. At some point
we'll sit down and filter
our notes – sift through the flotsam

to distil the pure, forward-facing
thoughts into a piece of work.
But not today.

THE REPTILE HOUSE

The highly sensitive person at the zoo
      recalls the throb of a dead arm
and avoids the reptile house—
      stench of hot sawdust,
raw existences dripping from the trees,
      oh hateful—the black beads
reminding her of love.

      And one day
when the bite comes she'll hate
      that also, desiring
outrageously to go on
      and on.

THE GREAT DISAPPOINTMENT

After Mary left, we waited
for another well-dressed lady

with a magic handbag to render it
OK. Several candidates

passed through, arriving by bus or by car, but none
appeared to know to bring the bag; situations

arose in which the items we needed
couldn't be found. Some had a distracted

air, as though they'd lost something
but couldn't remember what, glancing

always slightly to the side of where we
stood. Others checked their phones constantly,

as though they themselves were waiting to be rescued.
One even cried.

This was the great disappointment
of our lives: not the fact of our abandonment

by Mary, but the realisation, in view of the data,
that perhaps we'd only dreamt her.

THAT

It would be better not to be
that fly – the fly that sees
in stereo
what happens
that day

and, for that matter, all the days
before and after that.
The problem for
the fly is
that that

wall is too close to other walls,
producing that effect
of entrapment
one feels in
a box

that's been shut without a plan for
who will open it and
when. *Is that my
head?* wonders
the fly,

hearing thoughts tick like an heirloom
in a room where the big
light's been left on
by mistake –
like that,

like that, like that, like that, like that,
like that, like that, like that,
like that, like that,
like that, like
that, like

THE GARDEN

I can't turn away
from the yew hedge – not since

a squirrel shot in, full-
tilt, and the white cat,

which mewed as it rubbed
against my ankles, shot in after.

I heard the squirrel chirp –
war cry? surrender? –

and I've heard the phrase
she's a hunter

and of the gifts laid in fealty
on doormats and pillows.

I want no gifts today,
no half-murdered plaything

dropped panting and blinking
at my sandalled feet.

I walked into this
garden in innocence.

THE DRUM

How easy it would be to get a pan and a wooden spoon
and strip off, or simply not get dressed!

I'd march around the house all day, banging my drum.
It would be my house then. No room for you,

with your jumpers and papers and laptops and screens
and coffee cups ringing the desk with stains.

You'd stand in the doorway, hands over ears,
panicky and powerless to make it stop.

I don't care what you think, so why don't I do it?
Because I'm afraid of loneliness, and cold.

MULTIVERSE VALENTINE

In your lit eyes I see
other candles,
other flames.

On the stiff white tablecloth
I lay out my jokes
like the contents of a handbag.

Your laugh,
as mine, sounds
far away. But the scene –

how close and familiar it all is.
Uncountable
sweetnesses, tragedies.

WHAT MOUSE SAID

always looking for
tidy not scattered if
tunnelling to sniff
preen or dirty in
darktimes so eat it
away mess and tiny
enough to squeeze
skullhole make
neatnest if necessary
chew don't stop often
when smallmouths
turn out lick run
freeze crumbs keep
filing for what skirt
quick edgeways see
poorer in daylight

BUTTERMERE

All day I have sat on the lakebed
looking up at the undersides of clouds.
Here and not here.

The lake says there's nothing
to lose anymore.
The water is extremely clear.

JOINING THE SPIDERS

Caught out in the wrong shoes,
I choose to join the spiders
in a crevice in the old park wall.

To them, all weather
is the same; all time
is time to do some work.

I watch them working, watch
their old webs breathing
as I breathe, now tilting brickwards,

now tilting back, laced
with shreds of sycamore
and pigeon down. I wonder

if I stay here long enough
might they take me in –
reduce me

to a crescent of fingernail,
a snatch of hair – induct me
to their way of being there, stoically

sticking to one thing.
Then a robin
cocks his little head as if to query

why I'm crouched here like a toad
when the rain has stopped
and all these worms are ours for the taking.

ENTROPY

I find at the back of the freezer
a slice of sponge cake bagged and labelled
by your sweet, sure hands. Nothing ever

really dies: all the pieces of you
persist, riven and reconfigured
in infinite unknowable ways

and an unpredictable *drip, drip*
of knowable ones, astonishing
gifts, like this frozen wedge of time I

could pick up and feel the weight of, but
don't, because I know now that touching
something changes it.

HAWARDEN PARK, DAWN

Hammock of mercury
this snail's tell-tale,
strung five-cornered
between spears of grass.

Quietness, vast:
the dwindling millstream
and chatter of small throats
mere compass points.

In these moments
it isn't the heart we feel
unclenching
but the solar plexus –

a wild iris,
native of the forest floor,
loosening
as something dawns.

Oh stay like this, won't you –
expanding like the sky,
which only appears blue
distantly.

NOTES AND ACKNOWLEDGEMENTS

'Women Poets (in Order of Preference)' riffs on 'the three basic stereotypes of the woman poet' discussed by Jeni Couzyn in her introduction to *The Bloodaxe Book of Contemporary Women Poets* (1985).

'OM' is gardeners' shorthand for organic matter.

Versions of some of these poems were previously published in *Anthropocene*, *Bad Lilies*, *bath magg*, *Magma*, *PN Review*, *The Spectator* and *The Tangerine*.

I am grateful to Gladstone's Library for a Writers-in-Residence Award in May 2022; the poems I wrote there set the tone for this collection. I am also indebted to the Society of Authors for an Authors' Foundation Award for Works in Progress in 2020, and to Arts Council England for a DYCP award in 2021-22, both of which supported other creative endeavours that fed back into these poems.

Love and thanks to James Richards, Penny Boxall, Adam Crothers and Claudine Toutoungi for their generosity, encouragement and invaluable insights. Huge thanks also to Michael Schmidt, John McAuliffe and the team at Carcanet for everything they do.